BEFORE
I DIE

The simple, definitive guide to preserving your wishes,
telling your story, and documenting your financial, health,
and legal matters before the final sunset

Published by Mynd Matters Publishing
www.myndmatterspublishing.com

978-1-957092-89-8 (pbk)
978-1-957092-90-4 (hdc)

FIRST EDITION

ABOUT THIS GUIDE

Death, with its profound finality and emotional weight, often catches us off guard, leaving survivors with a plethora of detailed tasks and decisions that must be made in the midst of grief and confusion.

The heartfelt urgency that surrounds the topic of end-of-life planning and care for aging parents or loved ones is the impetus for this guide. It's a subject that, for the most part, does not occupy much space in our daily thoughts. We tend to focus on the immediate tasks at hand rather than contemplating the inevitable end of life.

Before I Die is a toolkit designed to capture your wishes and vital information to assist you and your loved ones through the sunset of your life. While it may be more convenient to skip or avoid certain pages, it is imperative to take the time to ensure you have gathered the right information. This preparation can make all the difference in facing whatever challenges may come.

Please remember that this guide will contain sensitive information. Therefore, it is essential to guard this information and keep it in a safe and secure location.

This guide is not just about preparing for the end. It is about empowering you to write your own story.

ABOUT THE CREATORS

In 2020, **Kelli Richardson Lawson** found herself experiencing a challenging journey with her eldest son, working through depression and addiction. With years of experience championing change and creating purpose initiatives like the CROWN Movement, Rap-It-Up, and the BET Summer Camp for Girls, this event changed the harmonious family dynamic into a whirlwind of chaos and heartbreak. Driven by her deep compassion for mental wellness and addiction issues, Kelli established **The SonRise Project**, a non-profit organization dedicated to supporting parents facing these challenges with their children. Anchored in her family values, Kelli hosts weekly support group calls, providing a nurturing and inspiring space for parents to connect, share experiences, and offer encouragement. These calls have become a lifeline, fostering understanding, compassion, and resilience in adversity.

Recognizing the life-changing potential of this initiative, the Oprah Winfrey Network collaborated with Kelli to create The SonRise Project podcast series, amplifying its reach to a nationwide audience in 2021.

In 2022, The SonRise Project extended its impact through specialized sessions called "SonRise to Sunset," a unique support group session on aging parents and the caregiving journey of our elders in their "sunset" years.

In early 2022, after losing her father, **Shewonia Y Roberts** was a guest speaker on the SonRise Project, sharing her knowledge and heartfelt story of loss and her journey with her mother, who has cognitive decline (dementia and Alzheimer's disease).

Shewonia shared invaluable lessons and lived experiences with the audience, and many callers wanted more information, advice, and help. That session inspired the creation of a comprehensive and loving space to discuss end-of-life planning, habits, financial/legal matters, and wishes.

How do you want to be remembered?

MY STORY

What would you want family/friends to say about you? Write your message to your family.
Remember to make this message inspiring to assist your loved ones with managing your mortality.

....

....

....

....

....

....

....

....

....

....

....

....

....

....

....

Date Completed

....

MY STORY: BELIEFS & VALUES

What words would you use to describe yourself?

....

....

....

....

....

What are some of your favorite sayings or quotes?
Tell your story by sharing more. Where did they come from? (My grandmother would say...)

....

....

....

....

....

....

....

....

....

....

MY STORY: EARLY YEARS

Write your story. *Include any associations, friends, teachers, and experiences that had a lasting impact.*

EDUCATIONAL INFORMATION

Elementary School and Years Attended
....

....

Do you have any special memories from elementary school?
....

....

....

....

Middle School and Years Attended
....

....

Do you have any special memories from middle school?
....

....

....

....

High School and Years Attended
....

....

Do you have any special memories from high school?
....

....

....

MY STORY: EARLY YEARS

EDUCATIONAL INFORMATION

Did you complete any internships or apprenticeships?

Did you learn any languages during your education?

List any scholarships, awards, or recognition you received during your education:

What extracurricular activities did you do during your education?

Do you have any special memories of them?

MY STORY: EARLY YEARS

Did you know what profession you wanted to work in when you finished high school?

....

....

What was it, and why did you find it appealing?

....

....

College/University, Degree Awarded, and Years Attended

....

....

How did you choose your college/university?

....

....

How did you choose your degree?

....

....

Did you join any clubs or organizations, like a sorority or fraternity? If so, which one(s)?

....

....

MY STORY: EARLY YEARS

EDUCATIONAL INFORMATION

Did you have any roommates during college/university? If so, who were they?

....

....

....

....

Do you have any special memories from college/university?

....

....

....

....

....

....

....

....

....

....

MY HABITS & PREFERENCES

Use this section to record your habits, quirks, and specific details about your daily routine.

PERSONAL HABITS & PRODUCT PREFERENCES	
Morning/Wake Up Routine	
Evening/Bedtime Routine	
Soap/Bath/Shower Gel	
Shampoo/Conditioner	
Other Hair Products	
Facial Moisturizer	
Facial Cleanser	
Sunscreen	
Toothpaste	
Shaving Cream	
Razor	
Aftershave/Perfume	
Lotion or Body Oil	
Lip Balm	
Deodorant	
Washing Detergent	
Make-up	
Nightwear	
Cologne or Perfume *(favorite scent)*	

MY HABITS & PREFERENCES

Be specific so family, friends, and caregivers know your detailed preferences.
Provide insights on how you like your meals prepared, favorite brands, etc.

MEALS, BEVERAGES, & SPECIAL REQUIREMENTS	
Favorite Breakfast	
Favorite Lunch	
Favorite Dinner	
Favorite Special Event Meal	
Favorite Fruit	
Favorite Vegetable	
Favorite Side Dish	
Favorite Dessert	
Favorite Drink	
Favorite Restaurant(s)	
Dislikes	
Allergies/Special Requirements	

MY HABITS & PREFERENCES

Questions listed are not comprehensive. If you have specific memories you would like to share or preferences that are not mentioned, write them in this space or attach additional pages.

PERSONAL INFORMATION

Name   Previous Name(s)

Social Security Number   Driver's License Number/ State

Date of Birth   Place of Birth

Current Address (Primary)   City   State / Zip code

Mobile Number

Place of Employment   Work Contact Name / Number

Citizenship / Visa / Naturalization Number   Military Affiliation / Status / Branch

Spouse / Partner

Marital Status   Spouse's Name   Phone Number

Social Security Number   Driver's License Number/ State

Date of Birth   Place of Birth

Current Address   City   State / Zip code

Mobile Number

Place of Employment   Work Contact Name / Number

Citizenship / Visa / Naturalization Number   Military Affiliation / Status / Branch

PERSONAL INFORMATION

Child / Stepchild

Name   Spouse's Name (if applicable)

Social Security Number   Driver's License Number/ State

Date of Birth   Place of Birth

Current Address   City   State / Zip code

Email Address(es)   Mobile Number

Place of Employment   Work Contact Name / Number

Citizenship / Visa / Naturalization Number   Military affiliation / Status / Branch

Guardian   Guardian's Phone Number

Child / Stepchild

Name   Spouse's Name (if applicable)

Social Security Number   Driver's License Number/ State

Date of Birth   Place of Birth

Current Address   City   State / Zip code

Email Address(es)   Mobile Number

Place of Employment   Work Contact Name / Number

Citizenship / Visa / Naturalization Number   Military affiliation / Status / Branch

Guardian   Guardian's Phone Number

PERSONAL INFORMATION

Child / Stepchild

Name

Spouse's Name (if applicable)

Social Security Number

Driver's License Number/ State

Date of Birth

Place of Birth

Current Address

City

State / Zip code

Email Address(es)

Mobile Number

Place of Employment

Work Contact Name / Number

Citizenship / Visa / Naturalization Number

Military affiliation / Status / Branch

Guardian

Guardian's Phone Number

Grandchild

Name

Spouse's Name (if applicable)

Social Security Number

Driver's License Number/ State

Date of Birth

Place of Birth

Current Address

City

State / Zip code

Email Address(es)

Mobile Number

Place of Employment

Work Contact Name / Number

Citizenship / Visa / Naturalization Number

Military affiliation / Status / Branch

Guardian

Guardian's Phone Number

PERSONAL INFORMATION

Grandchild

Name .... Spouse's Name (if applicable) ....

Social Security Number .... Driver's License Number/ State ....

Date of Birth .... Place of Birth ....

Current Address .... City .... State / Zip code ....

Email Address(es) .... Mobile Number ....

Place of Employment .... Work Contact Name / Number ....

Citizenship / Visa / Naturalization Number .... Military affiliation / Status / Branch ....

Guardian .... Guardian's Phone Number ....

Grandchild

Name .... Spouse's Name (if applicable) ....

Social Security Number .... Driver's License Number/ State ....

Date of Birth .... Place of Birth ....

Current Address .... City .... State / Zip code ....

Email Address(es) .... Mobile Number ....

Place of Employment .... Work Contact Name / Number ....

Citizenship / Visa / Naturalization Number .... Military affiliation / Status / Branch ....

Guardian .... Guardian's Phone Number ....

PERSONAL INFORMATION

Identify your maternal or paternal siblings, whether biological or otherwise.

Siblings

Name .... Mobile Number .... Email Address

Name .... Mobile Number .... Email Address

Name .... Mobile Number .... Email Address

Name .... Mobile Number .... Email Address

Name .... Mobile Number .... Email Address

Name .... Mobile Number .... Email Address

Name .... Mobile Number .... Email Address

Pets/Animals

NAME CHIP ID/REGISTRATION	DESCRIPTION	FEEDING SCHEDULE	VETERINARIAN'S CONTACT INFORMATION

Desired placement: ....

....

19

PERSONAL INFORMATION: YOUR DIGITAL LIFE
EMAIL & SOCIAL MEDIA

EMAIL ADDRESS	PASSWORD

SOCIAL MEDIA	USERNAME	PASSWORD

Instructions:

Instructions:

Instructions:

Instructions:

Instructions:

Instructions:

PERSONAL INFORMATION: YOUR DIGITAL STORY

*List the access information for all electronic devices
(e.g., computers, laptops, cell phones, tablets, e-readers, etc.).*

DEVICE	LOGIN/USER NAME	PASSWORD/HINT	NOTES

PERSONAL INFORMATION:
ACCOUNTS & LOYALTY PROGRAMS

Organization / Social Club

Organization / Social Club

Organizations / Social Club

Organization / Professional Club

Organization / Professional Club

Fitness Club / Gym

Fitness Club / Gym

Fitness Club / Gym

Wellness Center / Spa

Country Club / Golf Club

Other:

PERSONAL INFORMATION: MEMBERSHIPS

Document the information for your Airlines, Resorts/Hotels, Rental Cars, Grocery Stores, and other programs.

LOYALTY PROGRAM	USERNAME	LOYALTY #	PASSWORD
Airline			
Airline			
Airline			
Resort/ Hotel			
Resort/ Hotel			
Resort/ Hotel			
Rental Car			
Rental Car			
Pharmacy			
Pharmacy			
Grocery			
Retail Store			

ADVANCE CARE PLANNING

If I am hospitalized or in a nursing facility or at the time of my death, please honor these wishes. Here is a list of common documents to consider. Depending on your situation, you may choose to prepare with different documents.

DO NOT CALL / DO NOT ACCEPT CALLS FROM	DO NOT ALLOW VISITS FROM
Name	Name
Relationship	Relationship
Name	Name
Relationship	Relationship
Name	Name
Relationship	Relationship

IMPORTANT DOCUMENTS

Living Will	☐ Completed	☐ Drafted	☐ On My To-Do List		☐ N/A
Will	☐ Completed	☐ Drafted	☐ On My To-Do List		☐ N/A
Trust	☐ Completed	☐ Drafted	☐ On My To-Do List		☐ N/A
Power of Attorney	☐ Executive	☐ Medical	☐ Financial	☐ Digital	☐ N/A
Health/Medical Directive	☐ Completed	☐ Drafted	☐ On My To-Do List		☐ N/A
Burial, Funeral, Memorial Plans	☐ Completed	☐ Drafted	☐ On My To-Do List		☐ N/A
Guardianship	☐ Completed	☐ Drafted	☐ On My To-Do List	☐ Letter of Wishes	☐ N/A
....	☐ Completed	☐ Drafted	☐ On My To-Do List		☐ N/A

Seek legal advice when drafting these documents.
*A **Living Will** details your preferences for medical care while you are still alive and possibly unable to communicate.*
*A **Will** outlines how your assets will be distributed.*
*An **Advanced Health / Medical Directive** is a set of directions that outline your healthcare wishes.*

ADVANCE CARE PLANNING

Select your level of Importance for the listed medical situations.

MEDICAL SITUATION	NOT IMPORTANT	MODERATELY IMPORTANT	VERY IMPORTANT
Being at Home When I Die	☐	☐	☐
Being in the Hospital When I Die	☐	☐	☐
Being Alert	☐	☐	☐
Being Around My Family and Close Friends	☐	☐	☐
Being Able to Tell My Life Story and Leave Good Memories for Others	☐	☐	☐
Having Religious or Spiritual Advisors at My Side When I Die	☐	☐	☐
Reconciling Differences and Saying Good-bye to My Family and Friends	☐	☐	☐
Staying Alive Long Enough for My Family to Get to My Bedside Before I Die, Even If I'm Unconscious	☐	☐	☐

Other/Comments

....

....

....

....

....

....

ADVANCE CARE PLANNING

Document your preferences in the event you are at any point unable to speak for yourself.

CONSIDERATIONS	I WANT LIFE-SUSTAINING TREATMENTS	I DO NOT WANT LIFE-SUSTAINING TREATMENTS	DEPENDS ON THE CIRCUMSTANCES
If I am unconscious, in a coma, or in a vegetative state and there is little or no chance of recovery Comments/Clarifications:	☐	☐	☐
If I have permanent, severe brain damage that makes me unable to recognize my family or friends (e.g. severe Dementia) Comments/Clarifications:	☐	☐	☐
If I have a permanent condition where other people must help me with my daily routine and health needs (e.g. eating, bathing, movement) Comments/Clarifications:	☐	☐	☐
If I need to use a breathing machine and be in bed for the rest of my life Comments/Clarifications:	☐	☐	☐
If I have a pain or other severe symptoms that cause suffering and can't be relieved Comments/Clarifications:	☐	☐	☐
If I have a condition that will make me die very soon, even with life-sustaining treatments Comments/Clarifications:	☐	☐	☐

ADVANCE CARE PLANNING

Check the box for the statement that best aligns with your wishes.

I would always want my doctor to use medical treatments to prolong my life as long as possible, no matter the situation.

☐ This is my view

There might be some situations in which I would not want my doctor to use medical treatments to prolong my life.

☐ This is my view

There are definitely some situations in which I would not want my doctor to use medical treatments to prolong my life.

☐ This is my view

What are your religious beliefs that influence your medical views and treatment?
....
....
....
....

The following treatments should be considered as part of my care:
....
....
....
....
....
....
....

ADVANCE CARE PLANNING

Write down your wishes and preferences for where you would like to live as you grow older.

☐ Age in Place ☐ Independent Living ☐ Assisted Living ☐ Retirement Community
☐ Move in with Family ☐ Private Care Home ☐ Other ....

....

....

....

....

....

....

....

....

....

....

....

....

....

....

....

ADVANCE CARE PLANNING

The items below can be found in the listed locations.

Adoption Papers	
Anatomical Gift Information	
Appraisals	
Birth Certificate	
Divorce Decree	
Employment Noncompete	
Global Entry Card	
Marriage Certificate	
Military Records	
Motor Vehicle Titles	
Naturalization Papers	
Organ Donation	
Passport(s)	
Patents	
Prenuptial Agreements	
Property Title(s)/Deed(s)	
Real Estate Deeds	
Safe Deposit Box/Bank Name/Key Location	
Social Security Card	
Tax Returns (Federal and State)	
Trust Agreement	
VISA	

AT THE TIME OF MY PASSING

Insurance Policy for Funeral/Burial Expenses

....

....

Location
....

Contact information
....

Invitees	☐ Public	☐ Private	Notes ....
Viewing, Visitation, or Wake	☐ Yes	☐ No	Notes ....
Publish My Obituary	☐ Yes	☐ No	Notes ....

Type of Service   ☐ Burial   ☐ Cremation   ☐ Green Burial

Eulogy

Name   Contact information   Relationship

....

....

| BURIAL DETAILS ONLY |
| *Check one option from each column* |

| ☐ Immediate | ☐ Embalm | ☐ In-ground | ☐ Body Present |
| ☐ After Service | ☐ Do Not Embalm | ☐ Above Ground | ☐ Body Not Present |

CASKET

| ☐ Wood | ☐ Metal | ☐ Other |

AT THE TIME OF MY PASSING

Burial Attire

Clothing
....
....

Shoes
....

Accessories
....
....

Other items
....
....

Headstone or marker:　☐　Yes　☐　No

Description or material preference:

....

....

CREMATION DETAILS ONLY
Check one option from each column

☐ Immediate

☐ After Service　　　☐ Do Not Embalm

☐ In-ground

☐ Scattered

☐ Given to an Individual

Who ....

AT THE TIME OF MY PASSING

Program details; capture the song, artist, and location in the program.

Musical Selection(s) / Artist(s)

NAME OF SONG/ARTIST	WHERE (video, recessional, processional, etc.)

Readings (Scripture, Poem, etc.)

SPEAKER	TYPE OF READING

CONTACT LIST/MY VILLAGE

Write the contact information for the people closest to you—family, friends, mentors, colleagues, neighbors, civic and social orgs, volunteer orgs, and boards.
Note: There is a separate section for Financial and Legal resources.

NAME	RELATIONSHIP	PHONE NUMBER

CONACT LIST

CONTACT LIST/MY VILLAGE

Write the contact information for the people closest to you—family, friends, mentors, colleagues, neighbors, civic and social orgs, volunteer orgs, and boards.
Note: There is a separate section for Financial and Legal resources.

NAME	RELATIONSHIP	PHONE NUMBER

CONTACT LIST/ADVISORS

List the contact information for relevant legal, financial, and trusted administrative personnel.

EXECUTOR OF ESTATE

Name

Mobile #

Office #

Email

Mailing Address

ATTORNEY

Name

Mobile #

Office #

Email

Mailing Address

ACCOUNTANT

Name

Mobile #

Office #

Email

Mailing Address

CONTACT LIST/ADVISORS

List the contact information for relevant legal, financial, religious, and trusted administrative personnel.

FINANCIAL ADVISOR

Name

Mobile #

Office #

Email

Mailing Address

TAX PREPARER

Name

Mobile #

Office #

Email

Mailing Address

MINISTER/CLERGY/PASTOR

Name

Mobile #

Office #

Email

Mailing Address

FINANCIAL INFORMATION: BANKING

Financial Institution ....

Account Type (Deposit/Savings/Credit)   Account/Card Number   Exp. Date / Sec Code

....

Name (as it appears on account/card)   Sole or Joint Ownership (Name)   Email Address

....

Website   Username   Password

....

Account Type (Deposit/Savings/Credit)   Account Number   Exp. Date / Sec Code

....

Name (as it appears on account)   Sole or Joint Ownership (Name)   Email Address

....

Website   Username   Password

....

ATM Card

Card Number   Exp Date / Sec Code

....

Other Notes:

....

FINANCIAL INFORMATION: BANKING

Financial Institution ....

Account Type (Deposit/Savings/Credit)	Account/Card Number	Exp. Date / Sec Code
....	....	....
Name (as it appears on account/card)	Sole or Joint Ownership (Name)	Email Address
....	....	....
Website	Username	Password
....	....	....

Account Type (Deposit/Savings/Credit)	Account Number	Exp. Date / Sec Code
....	....	....
Name (as it appears on account)	Sole or Joint Ownership (Name)	Email Address
....	....	....
Website	Username	Password
....	....	....

ATM Card

Card Number   Exp Date / Sec Code

....

Other Notes:

....

FINANCIAL INFORMATION: BANKING

Financial Institution ....

Account Type (Deposit/Savings/Credit)	Account/Card Number	Exp. Date / Sec Code
....	....	....

Name (as it appears on account/card)	Sole or Joint Ownership (Name)	Email Address
....	....	....

Website	Username	Password
....	....	....

Account Type (Deposit/Savings/Credit)	Account Number	Exp. Date / Sec Code
....	....	....

Name (as it appears on account)	Sole or Joint Ownership (Name)	Email Address
....	....	....

Website	Username	Password
....	....	....

ATM Card

Card Number	Exp Date / Sec Code
....	....

Other Notes:

....

FINANCIAL INFORMATION: BANKING

Financial Institution ....

Account Type (Deposit/Savings/Credit)	Account/Card Number	Exp. Date / Sec Code
....	....	....
Name (as it appears on account/card)	Sole or Joint Ownership (Name)	Email Address
....	....	....
Website	Username	Password
....	....	....

Account Type (Deposit/Savings/Credit)	Account Number	Exp. Date / Sec Code
....	....	....
Name (as it appears on account)	Sole or Joint Ownership (Name)	Email Address
....	....	....
Website	Username	Password
....	....	....

ATM Card

Card Number	Exp Date / Sec Code
....	....

Other Notes:

....

FINANCIAL INFORMATION: CREDIT CARDS

Credit Card Provider

....

Name (as it appears on card)

....

Website

....

Account Number

....

Sole or Joint Ownership (Name)

....

Username

....

Exp. / Sec Code

....

Email Address

....

Password

....

Credit Card Provider

....

Name (as it appears on card)

....

Website

....

Account Number

....

Sole or Joint Ownership (Name)

....

Username

....

Exp. / Sec Code

....

Email Address

....

Password

....

Credit Card Provider

....

Name (as it appears on card)

....

Website

....

Account Number

....

Sole or Joint Ownership (Name)

....

Username

....

Exp. / Sec Code

....

Email Address

....

Password

....

FINANCIAL INFORMATION: CREDIT CARDS

Credit Card Provider	Account Number	Exp. / Sec Code
....	....	....
Name (as it appears on card)	Sole or Joint Ownership (Name)	Email Address
....	....	....
Website	Username	Password
....	....	....

Credit Card Provider	Account Number	Exp. / Sec Code
....	....	....
Name (as it appears on card)	Sole or Joint Ownership (Name)	Email Address
....	....	....
Website	Username	Password
....	....	....

Credit Card Provider	Account Number	Exp. / Sec Code
....	....	....
Name (as it appears on card)	Sole or Joint Ownership (Name)	Email Address
....	....	....
Website	Username	Password
....	....	....

FINANCIAL INFORMATION: STORE CARDS

Card Provider

....

Name (as it appears on card)

....

Website

....

Account Number

....

Sole or Joint Ownership (Name)

....

Username

....

Exp. / Sec Code

....

Email Address

....

Password

....

Card Provider

....

Name (as it appears on card)

....

Website

....

Account Number

....

Sole or Joint Ownership (Name)

....

Username

....

Exp. / Sec Code

....

Email Address

....

Password

....

Card Provider

....

Name (as it appears on card)

....

Website

....

Account Number

....

Sole or Joint Ownership (Name)

....

Username

....

Exp. / Sec Code

....

Email Address

....

Password

....

FINANCIAL INFORMATION

PENSION

Account Number

Bank / Institution

Username   Password / PIN

401(K) / RETIREMENT ACCOUNT

Account Number

Bank / Institution

Username   Password / PIN

INVESTMENT ACCOUNT

Account Number

Bank / Institution

Username   Password / PIN

INVESTMENT ACCOUNT

Account Number

Bank / Institution

Username   Password / PIN

FINANCIAL INFORMATION

INVESTMENT ACCOUNT

Account Number

Bank / Institution

Username   Password / PIN

MUTUAL FUNDS

Account Number

Bank / Institution

Username   Password / PIN

CONTINGENT INTEREST

Account Number

Bank / Institution

Username   Password / PIN

529 PLAN

Account Number

Bank / Institution

Username   Password / PIN

FINANCIAL INFORMATION

CERTIFICATE OF DEPOSITS

Account Number

Bank / Institution

Username   Password / PIN

FLEXIBLE SPENDING ACCOUNT (FSA)

Account Number

Bank / Institution

Username   Password / PIN

RESTRICTED STOCK OPTIONS

Account Number

Bank / Institution

Username   Password / PIN

STOCK OPTIONS

Account Number

Bank / Institution

Username   Password / PIN

FINANCIAL INFORMATION

OTHER ACCOUNT

Account Number

Bank / Institution

Username   Password / PIN

OTHER ACCOUNT

Account Number

Bank / Institution

Username   Password / PIN

OTHER ACCOUNT

Account Number

Bank / Institution

Username   Password / PIN

OTHER ACCOUNT

Account Number

Bank / Institution

Username   Password / PIN

FINANCIAL INFORMATION: BUSINESS OWNERSHIP

Name of Business

....

Business Address

....

Lease/Own Location

....

# of Employees

....

Tax ID #

....

% Interest

....

Business Accountant

....

Business Attorney

....

Partners/Other Owners

....

Location of Ownership Documents

....

Date of Ownership or Incorporation

....

State of Incorporation

....

Social Media Accounts

....

....

....

Website

....

Website Designer

....

Other Information (List additional details including the type of business (e.g., LLC, Corporation, Not-for-Profit), net worth, and evaluation date)

....

....

....

....

....

FINANCIAL INFORMATION: VEHICLES

Owner / Lien Holder

....

Make / Model / Year

....

Account #

....

VIN / ID

....

Sole or Joint Ownership

....

Color

....

Website

....

Username

....

Password

....

Owner / Lien Holder

....

Make / Model / Year

....

Account #

....

VIN / ID

....

Sole or Joint Ownership

....

Color

....

Website

....

Username

....

Password

....

Owner / Lien Holder

....

Make / Model / Year

....

Account #

....

VIN / ID

....

Sole or Joint Ownership

....

Color

....

Website

....

Username

....

Password

....

FINANCIAL INFORMATION: OTHER VEHICLES

Boat

Owner / Lien Holder	Make / Model	HIN / ID
....	....	....

Year	Current Location	
....	....	

Motorcycle

Owner / Lien Holder	Make / Model	VIN / ID
....	....	....

Year	Current Location	
....	....	

Bicycle

Brand	Model	VIN / ID
....	....	....

Color	Year	Location
....	....	....

FINANCIAL INFORMATION: REAL ESTATE

REAL ESTATE (Primary)

Title Owner and/or Lender	Account / Loan Number
Property Address	
Monthly Payment Amount	Purchase Date/ Original Price
Website	Username / Password

REAL ESTATE (Other Property)

Title Owner and/or Lender	Account / Loan Number
Property Address	
Monthly Payment Amount	Purchase Date/ Original Price
Website	Username / Password

REAL ESTATE (Other Property)

Title Owner and/or Lender	Account / Loan Number
Property Address	
Monthly Payment Amount	Purchase Date/ Original Price
Website	Username / Password

FINANCIAL INFORMATION: ASSETS & PERSONAL PROPERTY

Add other items that were not captured on previous pages (e.g., personal loans extended to others, co-signer on an agreement, etc.)

ITEM	LOCATION	NOTES

FINANCIAL INFORMATION: LOANS

Student/Parent Loans

Lender   Account / Loan Number

Parent or Student

Website   Username / Password

Lender   Account / Loan Number

Parent or Student

Website   Username / Password

401K Loan / Other Loans / Lines of Credit

Lender   Account Loan Number

Website   Username / Password

Lender   Account Loan Number

Website   Username / Password

Lender   Account Loan Number

Website   Username / Password

FINANCIAL INFORMATION

FINANCIAL INFORMATION: INCOME SOURCES

INCOME SOURCE	PROVIDER
Primary Income	
Secondary Income	
Rental Income	
Board Position	
Social Security	
Food Assistance	
Veterans Benefits	
Pension/Retirement	
Fellowships / Stipends	
Annuity Programs	
Child Support	
Spousal Support / Alimony	

Other Income

FINANCIAL INFORMATION: HOUSEHOLD BILLS

ACCOUNT TYPE	PROVIDER	ACCOUNT #	USERNAME	PASSWORD	PIN

FINANCIAL INFORMATION:
SUBSCRIPTIONS AND STREAMING SERVICES

STREAMING PROVIDER/ SUBSCRIPTION SERVICE	EMAIL ADDRESS	USERNAME	PASSWORD	MONTHLY PAYMENT

INSURANCE INFORMATION

This section is for important information, including documents, insurance policies, property, and accounts.

MEDICAL INSURANCE *(Primary)*

Carrier ....

Member ID ....

Group # ....

Phone Number ....

Patient Website ....

Username ....

Password ....

MEDICAL INSURANCE *(Secondary)*

Carrier ....

Member ID ....

Group # ....

Phone Number ....

Patient Website ....

Username ....

Password ....

DENTAL INSURANCE

Carrier ....

Member ID ....

Group # ....

Phone Number ....

Patient Website ....

Username ....

Password ....

VISION INSURANCE

Carrier ....

Member ID ....

Group # ....

Phone Number ....

Patient Website ....

Username ....

Password ....

INSURANCE INFORMATION

This section is for important information, including documents, insurance policies, property, and accounts.

MEDICARE

Carrier ....

Member ID ....

Group # ....

Phone Number ....

Patient Website ....

Username ....

Password ....

MEDICAID

Carrier ....

Member ID ....

Group # ....

Phone Number ....

Patient Website ....

Username ....

Password ....

OTHER INSURANCE

Carrier ....

Member ID ....

Group # ....

Phone Number ....

Patient Website ....

Username ....

Password ....

OTHER INSURANCE

Carrier ....

Member ID ....

Group # ....

Phone Number ....

Patient Website ....

Username ....

Password ....

INSURANCE INFORMATION

LIFE INSURANCE	POLICY #	CONTACT NAME	PHONE NUMBER
....	....	....	....
....	....	....	....
		Contact	

LONG-TERM CARE INSURANCE	POLICY #	CONTACT NAME	PHONE NUMBER
....	....	....	....
		Contact	

HOMEOWNER'S INSURANCE	POLICY #	CONTACT NAME	PHONE NUMBER
....	....	....	....
		Contact	

RENTER'S INSURANCE	POLICY #	CONTACT NAME	PHONE NUMBER
....	....	....	....
		Contact	

PET INSURANCE	POLICY #	CONTACT NAME	PHONE NUMBER
....	....	....	....
		Contact	

INSURANCE INFORMATION

DISABILITY INSURANCE	POLICY #	CONTACT NAME	PHONE NUMBER
....	....	....	....

Contact ....

ACCIDENTAL DEATH & DISMEMBERMENT INSURANCE	POLICY #	CONTACT NAME	PHONE NUMBER
....	....	....	....

Contact ....

APPLIANCE INSURANCE	POLICY #	CONTACT NAME	PHONE NUMBER
....	....	....	....

Contact ....

VALUABLE ITEMS (Art, Jewelry, Antiques, etc.)	POLICY #	CONTACT NAME	PHONE NUMBER
....	....	....	....
....	....	....	....
....	....	....	....
....	....	....	....

Contact ....

MEDICAL INFORMATION

This section is for tracking your medical information. Include contact details for your medical personnel as well as a record of your medications, insurance policies, and any medical history you think is relevant.

Primary Care Physician   Phone Number

Facility Address/Portal Address   Username/Password

Dentist   Phone Number

Facility Address/Portal Address   Username/Password

Optometry/Ophthalmologist   Phone Number

Facility Address/Portal Address   Username/Password

Podiatrist   Phone Number

Facility Address   Username/Password

Chiropractor   Phone Number

Facility Address/Portal Address   Username/Password

Obstetrician/Gynecologist   Phone Number

Facility Address/Portal Address   Username/Password

Urologist   Phone Number

Facility Address/Portal Address   Username/Password

Acupuncturist   Phone Number

Facility Address/Portal Address   Username/Password

MEDICAL INFORMATION

This section is for tracking your medical information. Include contact details for your medical personnel as well as a record of your medications, insurance policies, and any medical history you think is relevant.

Geriatric Specialist
Phone Number

Facility Address/Portal Address
Username/Password

Oncologist
Phone Number

Facility Address/Portal Address
Username/Password

Cardiologist
Phone Number

Facility Address/Portal Address
Username/Password

Orthopedic
Phone Number

Facility Address/Portal Address
Username/Password

Therapist
Phone Number

Facility Address/Portal Address
Username/Password

Other
Phone Number

Facility Address/Portal Address
Username/Password

Other
Phone Number

Facility Address/Portal Address
Username/Password

Other
Phone Number

Facility Address/Portal Address
Username/Password

MEDICAL HISTORY

This section is for tracking your medical information. Include contact details for your medical personnel as well as a record of your medications, insurance policies, and any medical history you think is relevant. Medical history charts can be found at nationalbreastcancer.org.

CONDITION	YES	NO	IF YES, PROVIDE DETAILS.
Alcohol or drug abuse			
Allergies			
Anxiety			
Asthma			
Autoimmune disease (rheumatoid arthritis, psoriasis, multiple sclerosis, lupus, inflammatory bowel disease, celiac, etc.)			
Autism			
Birth defects (heart defects, spina bifida, etc.)			
Blood disease			
Bone and joint diseases			
Cancer			
Bladder			
Breast			
Cervical			
Colorectal (Colon)			
Esophageal			
Kidney			
Leukemia			
Liver			
Lung			
Lymphoma			
Ovarian			
Prostate			
Stomach (Gastric)			
Thyroid			
Depression			
Diabetes or insulin resistance (type 1, type 2, or pre-diabetic)			

MEDICAL HISTORY

This section is for tracking your medical information. Include contact details for your medical personnel as well as a record of your medications, insurance policies, and any medical history you think is relevant. Medical history charts can be found at nationalbreastcancer.org.

CONDITION	YES	NO	IF YES, PROVIDE DETAILS.
Epilepsy			
Gastrointestinal Disorder (Acid Reflux,Ulcer, Gastritis, Irritable Bowel Disorder)			
Glandular Disorder			
Hearing Loss			
Heart Disease (Including Heart Attack)			
Hemophilia			
High Blood Pressure			
High Cholesterol			
Infertility or Repeat Pregnancy Loss			
Intellectual Disabilities (Cerebral Palsy, Speech and Language Problems, etc.)			
Immunodeficiency Disorder (Strep throat, Mononucleosis, Hepatitis, HIV/AIDS, other)			
Kidney Condition			
Lung Disease (Pneumonia, Bronchitis, Asthma, Tuberculosis)			
Mental/psychotic disorder (Including Schizophrenia)			
Migraines			
Muscular Disease			
Nerve Disorder			
Ocular Disease			
Organ Transplants			
Pulmonary Embolism (PE)			
Sickle Cell Disease			
Spinal Muscular Atrophy			
Spleen Surgery			
Smoking Habits			
Skin Condition (Eczema, Psoriasis, Acne, Rosacea, Ichthyosis, Vitiligo, Hives, Seborrheic Dermatitis, etc.)			
Stroke			
Thalassemia (A type of Anemia)			
Vision Impairment			

MEDICAL HISTORY

Medical documentation and history are essential to everyone's care and treatment.

Major Hospitalizations, Surgeries, Blood Transfusions, and Other Procedures

DATE (MM/YYYY)	TYPE OF PROCEDURE	LOCATION	TREATING PHYSICIAN

Weight .... *Height* .... *ft* .... *inches*

Allergic or unusual reactions to:

☐ Nuts ☐ Gluten ☐ Dairy/Lactose ☐ Other ....

☐ Penicillin ☐ Latex ☐ Aspirin ☐ Other ....

SYMPTOMS

If a food allergen has been ingested, but no symptoms:

Mouth	*Itching, tingling, or swelling of lips*	☐Epinephrine	☐Antihistamine
Skin	*Hives, Itchy rash, swelling*	☐Epinephrine	☐Antihistamine
Other		☐Epinephrine	☐Antihistamine

MEDICAL HISTORY: IMMUNIZATION RECORDS

TYPE	YEAR	COMMENTS
COVID-19		
Diphtheria, Tetanus		
Hepatitis A		
Hepatitis B		
Human Papilloma Virus (HPV)		
Influenza		
Respiratory Syncytial Virus (RSV)		
Pneumococcal Vaccine		
RSV Respiratory Syncytial Virus		
Measles, Mumps & Rubella (MMR)		
Td/Tdap		
Varicella (Chickenpox)		
Other		
Other		
Other		
Other		

Are you a registered organ donor? ☐ Yes ☐ No

Notes: ....

....

MEDICATIONS/PRESCRIPTIONS

Tip: Take photos of medications, ensuring you can see the label and dosage clearly.

MEDICATIONS	PRESCRIBED BY	PURPOSE	DOSE/ FREQUENCY	NOTES:

MEDICAL
INFORMATION

MEDICAL HISTORY: FAMILY

Fill out the checklist below with your biological relative's medical history (living and deceased). Medical history charts can be found at nationalbreastcancer.org.

CONDITION	NO	MATERNAL	PATERNAL	MOTHER	FATHER	SIBLINGS	IF YES, PROVIDE DETAILS.
Alcohol or drug abuse							
Allergies							
Anxiety							
Asthma							
Autoimmune disease (rheumatoid arthritis, psoriasis, multiple sclerosis, lupus, inflammatory bowel disease, celiac, etc.)							
Autism							
Birth defects (heart defects, spina bifida, etc.)							
Blood disease							
Bone and joint diseases							
Cancer							
Bladder							
Breast							
Cervical							
Colorectal (Colon)							
Endometrial							
Esophageal							
Kidney							
Leukemia							
Liver							
Lung							
Lymphoma							

MEDICAL HISTORY: FAMILY

Fill out the checklist below with your biological relative's medical history (living and deceased). Medical history charts can be found at nationalbreastcancer.org.

CONDITION	NO	MATERNAL	PATERNAL	MOTHER	FATHER	SIBLINGS	IF YES, PROVIDE DETAILS.
Ovarian							
Prostate							
Stomach (Gastric)							
Thyroid							
Other:							
Depression							
Diabetes or insulin resistance (type 1, type 2, or pre-diabetic)							
Epilepsy							
Gastrointestinal disorder							
Glandular disorder							
Hearing loss							
Heart disease (including heart attack)							
Hemophilia							
High blood pressure							
High cholesterol							
Infertility or repeat pregnancy loss							
Intellectual disabilities (cerebral palsy, speech and language problems, etc.)							
Immunodeficiency Disorder							

Have you had any ancestral DNA analysis completed? ☐ Yes ☐ No

Comments about findings:

We Are
Who We Are,
Because You Are
Who You Are.

Continue to tell
your story.

MORE ABOUT ME

*Think about the stories you want your family and loved ones to remember.
Tell your story and include aspirations that you have/have not achieved.*

CREATIVE PURSUITS

Do you create art? If so, what media/style?

....

....

....

Do you have any photos of your work? *(Link or copy your photos here.)*

....

....

....

Can you play an instrument or sing? If so, which instrument or style?

....

....

....

What is your favorite song to perform?

....

....

....

Do you have a video of a performance? If so, where? *(Link or copy your video here.)*

....

....

....

Do you act or dance? If so, what style?

....

....

....

MORE ABOUT ME

FAVORITES

What is your favorite play (musical or opera) and why?

....

....

What is your favorite book and why?

....

....

What is your favorite game and why?

....

....

What are your favorite sports teams and why?

....

....

Who is your favorite athlete and why?

....

....

What is your favorite color and why?

....

....

MORE ABOUT ME

What was your favorite travel destination and why?

....

....

....

What are your hobbies?

....

....

....

Who is your all-time favorite musical artists and why?

....

....

....

What is your favorite song/album and why?

....

....

....

What is your favorite movie and why?

....

....

....

What is your favorite TV show and why?

....

....

....

MORE ABOUT ME

PROFESSIONAL BACKGROUND

What is your current/most recent job title?

Who is your current/most recent employer, and where are they?

What was your first job?

Where and when did you work there?

What other job titles have you held?

Where and when did you work there (for each)?

MORE ABOUT ME

How did you choose your career/industry?

....

....

....

What professional accomplishments are you most proud of?

....

....

....

What other accomplishments have you achieved during your career?

....

....

....

Are/were you involved in any professional organizations?

....

....

....

Did you hold any positions in your organization?

....

....

....

What are the skills you bring to your career?

....

....

MORE ABOUT ME

PROFESSIONAL BACKGROUND

What are the skills you bring to your career?

....

....

....

What is your favorite workplace memory?

....

....

....

Do you have any funny workplace stories?

....

....

....

What advice would you give someone working in your industry?

....

....

....

COMMUNITY / CHURCH ENGAGEMENT

Religion   **Church/ Synagogue /Temple**

....

....

....

MORE ABOUT ME: A MESSAGE TO MY FAMILY

Is there more to your story? Finish writing it here.

....

....

....

....

....

....

....

....

....

....

....

....

....

....

MORE
ABOUT ME

Home Evaluation & Environment Checklist For Caregivers

HOME EVALUATION & ENVIRONMENT CHECKLIST

Cognitive and physical decline brings with them several safety concerns. Use this checklist of common hazards to evaluate the safety of your or your loved ones' environment and their financial and medical situations. List any hazards and consider potential ways to remove or mitigate them.

This checklist is also useful for assessing the suitability of one's current environment to their care needs and should be used in preparation for making decisions about alternative or residential care provisions.

HOUSEHOLD	POTENTIAL ACTIONS

Stairs
Are the stairs easy to navigate up and down? Modify the stairs or install a chair lift

Are the stairs slippery? Place non-slip mats

Is there a handrail that is fit for purpose? Install a handrail

Shopping Habits
Are they purchasing unneeded items online?

Is the clutter affecting hygiene or sanitation?

Is there a risk of a fire (near the stacked or clutter items)?

Is there a risk of stacked clutter falling?

Are there firearms in the home?

A sprinkler system?

Fire extinguisher?

Are there accessible sharp objects?

Are there trip hazards (e.g., rugs on tile)?

Entrance & Exit
Are there steps at the entrance and exit to the home?

What is the process to open/lock the door?

Code, fob, keys

What is the best way to access the home. Front, back door?

Do you have a way to access the home if there is an accident?

Who else has a key or other access to the home?

Is there an alarm system?

Who is being called or alerted in the event of an alarm?

How many points of egress? Front door? Back Door? Others?

Household Maintenance
Are there any maintenance issues that need to be resolved?

Are your parents likely to attempt unsafe household maintenance?

Is the house a comfortable temperature?

How is this being controlled? App, manually?

HOME EVALUATION & ENVIRONMENT CHECKLIST

Finances

Financial Fundamentals
Have they lost a checkbook or credit/debit card/ATM card?

Are their bills being paid on time?

Are they able to afford necessities like food and medication?

Shopping Habits
Are they purchasing unneeded items online?

Are they going on unnecessary shopping sprees?

Are there bags of groceries/food in the house that have been purchased but not opened?

Scams, Crimes, & Financial Abuse
Have they been a victim of fraud or a scam?

Have they mentioned meeting someone, in person or online, that has asked them for money?

Have they received unexpected official-looking bills or notices, such as tax bills?

Have they loaned money to friends or family?

Have they been contacted by a stranger that claims to know them or be family?

Are there items missing from the home?

Are there suspicious marks on their house or car?

Have they changed their will or life insurance policies?

Daily Habits

Food & Eating Habits
Are they eating meals as they normally would?

Is there enough food in their home?

Is there spoiled or out-of-date food in their home?

Are the meals adequately/properly cooked?

Driving
Are there new or unexplained dents on their vehicle?

Have they had a car accident or increasing numbers of accidents?

Are the vehicles correctly maintained? Oil? Tire rotation? Charging station?

HOME EVALUATION & ENVIRONMENT CHECKLIST

Have you noticed unsafe driving habits, like not turning on headlights at night?

Are they able to safely navigate while driving?

Have they gotten lost along a familiar route?

Memory
Have they lost their car keys, house keys, or other important item?

Do they frequently misplace objects?

Have they gotten lost in their neighborhood?

Have they been found wandering in the neighborhood?

Have they forgotten to turn off the stove or iron?

Have they mistakenly gone to the wrong house or a previous address?

Do they struggle to remember important names or appointment dates?

Are there items missing from the home?

Are there suspicious marks on their house or car?

Have they changed their will or life insurance policies?

Personal Safety

Medical Safety
If they have prescription medications, are the medications secure?

Are they taking the medications in accordance with a doctor or nurse's instructions?

Do they have any untreated injuries?

Have they developed a limp or other affectation?

Have they mentioned unexplained pain?

Elder Abuse
Is your parent frightened of or unwilling to be alone with someone?

Do they have injuries they can't or won't explain?

Does your parent seem depressed or withdrawn?

Is your parent dehydrated or malnourished?

Do they seem isolated from friends and family?